Contents

PART 4: REAL-WORLD MONEY
How money shows up all around you...
and what you can do with it

Business Brain Challenge
Can You Make $10 from Scratch?

BACK POCKET BONUSES

GrowForth Kids Co.

HOW MONEY WORKS

Learn How to Earn It, Save It, Grow It, and Spend It Wisely

Matthew MacMillan and Scott MacMillan

GROW FORTH

PRESS
—BY GRAMMAR FACTORY—

Grow Forth Kids
MacMillan Company Limited
25 Telegram Mews, 39th Floor, Suite 3906
Toronto, Ontario, Canada
M5V 3Z1

www.growforthpress.com

MacMillan, Matthew and Scott MacMillan
GrowForth Kids Co: How Money Works: Learn how to earn it, save it, grow it, and spend it wisely / Matthew MacMillan and Scott MacMillan.

Paperback ISBN 978-1-998528-45-5
Hardcover ISBN 978-1-998528-46-2
eBook ISBN 978-1-998528-47-9

1. JNF013050 JUVENILE NONFICTION / Business & Economics / General.
2. JNF013030 JUVENILE NONFICTION / Business & Economics / Personal Finance.
3. JNF000000 JUVENILE NONFICTION / General.

Production Credits
Book production and editorial services by Grammar Factory (www.grammarfactory.com)

Introduction
Welcome to GrowForth Kids Co.

Hi there! 👋

We're so glad you're here.

Welcome to **GrowForth Kids Co.** – where curious kids like you learn how the world *really* works. Not just in fairy tales or cartoons, but in real life...with real money, real choices, and real ways to do something awesome with what you've got.

You might be wondering: **"Why should I care about money stuff? I'm a kid!"**

Well, here's the secret: You don't have to wait until you're a grown-up to think like one.

You already make money choices every day – like whether to spend your allowance, save up for something big, or trade your snack for a friend's at lunch (classic economic thinking!). You might even be thinking about starting a business someday. Or sooner. Like...next weekend.

This book is your *starter kit*. Inside, you'll learn:

- Where money comes from
- How to earn it, save it, and grow it
- What smart spenders think about before they buy
- And how to decide what matters most to *you*

Each chapter explains one important idea – in plain, kid-friendly language – with real-life examples and a little sketch to help you picture it. At the end of each one, there's a **"Try This!"** box with a small challenge you can try on your own or with a grown-up.

And when you've read the whole book?

You'll take on your first **GrowForth Kids Co. Business Brain Challenge.** (It's fun. Trust us.)

Let's get going. Your money brain is ready to grow forth.

Part 1

Money Basics

What money is, what it does, and why it matters

Money might seem like a bunch of coins, bills, or numbers on a screen – but it's actually one of the smartest tools humans have ever invented. It helps people exchange goods, make plans, measure value, and even take smart risks to build something bigger.

But before you start earning, spending, or growing money, there's something even more important: understanding what money really is. Where it came from. Why it works. And how it changes over time.

In this section, you'll learn:

- What money actually *is*, and how it replaced bartering (like trading goats for gumdrops)
- Why the *value* of something isn't always what it costs
- What *inflation* is, and why prices go up over time
- Why *waiting* to use your money can sometimes be the smartest move
- And how to think about *risk* in a way that helps – not hurts – your money goals

Let's unlock the basics behind every dollar, coin, or card in your pocket.

1

What Is Money?

From trading stuff to dollars and coins

What it means

Money is a tool we use to trade things. It helps people get what they need (or want) without having to swap stuff directly.

A long time ago, before money existed, people used **barter** – trading one thing for another. For example:

"I'll give you 5 apples if you fix my fence."

But what if the person fixing the fence didn't *want* apples? What if they wanted shoes instead?

That's where money comes in. Instead of trading stuff for stuff, people started using money as a **way to measure value**. You give someone money for their work or their things – then they can use that money to get what *they* want.

Here's an example

Imagine you make friendship bracelets and want to trade one with a friend who has stickers. She agrees and gives you 5 cool stickers. That's a trade.

But what if she doesn't want a bracelet? Or doesn't like the color?

Now imagine you sell your bracelet to someone else for $2 – and then use that $2 to buy the stickers from your friend. That's using **money** instead of bartering. Easier, right?

Why it's important

Money solves the problems of bartering – like not wanting the same thing, or not needing it right now. It makes trading easier and faster.

It also lets people **save** value for later, **compare** how valuable things are, and **buy** or **sell** from anyone – not just someone who wants to trade directly.

Try this!

Think of something you'd like to sell – it could be a drawing, a bookmark, or a snack (with permission!). Now imagine trying to trade it for something you want. Would that be easy or hard?

Then think: would using money make it easier?

USING MONEY INSTEAD OF BARTERING

Book Value vs. Market Value

What things are really worth

What it means

Not everything is worth exactly what it *says* it's worth.

Sometimes, people write down a number – like how much something *cost* to make or how much it was *originally* worth. That's called the **book value**.

But what someone is actually willing to *pay* for it right now? That's the **market value**.

Book value is like the official price. Market value is like what someone will really pay for it.

Here's an example

Imagine you have a backpack that cost $40 when it was new. That's its book value.

But now it has some doodles on it, one of the zippers sticks, and you've used it for two years. If you tried to sell it, someone might only want to pay $10. That's the market value.

Or... imagine it's a *rare* backpack with a cool patch from a special event, and a collector really wants it. Now they might pay **more** than the book value – maybe $60 or $70! That's also the market value.

Why it's important

Understanding the difference between book value and market value helps you:

- Know what something is really worth to others
- Avoid paying too much for something just because it's "expensive"
- Recognize when something you own is more valuable than you thought

This is how smart buyers (and sellers!) think.

Try this!

Pick 3 things you own – like a toy, a book, or a backpack.

Write down what you *think* they cost new (book value), and then ask:

- What would someone pay for this now?
- Is that more or less?

That's your **market value** guess.

3

Inflation

Why things cost more over time

What it means

Inflation is when prices go **up** over time – not because things got bigger or better, but because the **value of money went down** a little.

That means the same item that cost $1 a few years ago might cost $1.25 or $1.50 today. The money you saved still has the same number on it – but it doesn't buy as much as it used to.

Here's an example

Let's say your favorite snack used to cost **$2**. A year later, that same snack is **$2.25**, even though it looks exactly the same.

Why? That's inflation at work – the prices of things slowly rising over time.

And it's not just snacks. Inflation affects toys, clothes, school supplies, and even what adults pay for rent, gas, and groceries.

Why it's important

When you understand inflation, you can:

- See why saving money is good – but growing money is even better
- Understand why prices change from year to year
- Make smarter choices with your money, especially when planning for the future

Even grown-ups plan their lives and jobs around inflation. So knowing about it early? That's a money superpower.

Try this!

Ask a grown-up what their favorite snack or toy cost when *they* were your age. Then compare that to what it costs today. That's inflation – and now you've spotted it in the wild!

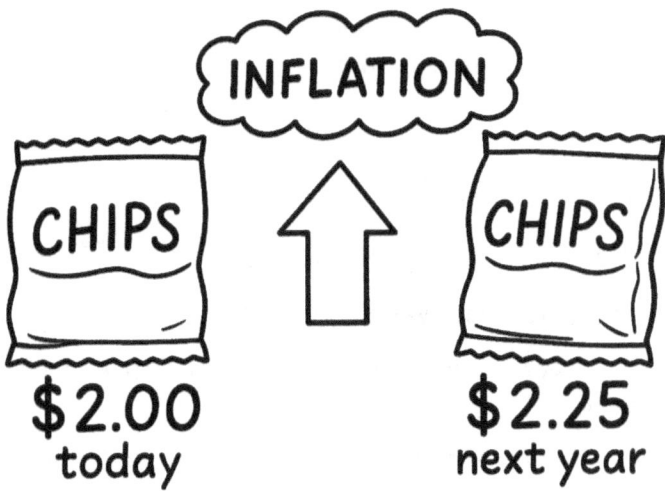

4

Time Value of Money
(aka Delayed Gratification)
Why waiting can be worth it

What it means

The **time value of money** means that a dollar today is usually worth more than a dollar tomorrow – because if you have it *now*, you can use it, grow it, or earn more from it.

Delayed gratification is a fancy way of saying: *"Wait now, enjoy more later."*

These two ideas go hand in hand – they both show that **patience can pay off** when it comes to money.

Here's an example

A long time ago, scientists gave kids a test.

They put one **marshmallow** on a table and said,

"You can eat this one marshmallow now... or if you wait 15 minutes, you'll get **two**."

Some kids waited (even though it was *really* hard). Some didn't.

The kids who waited? They didn't just get more marshmallows – later in life, they often made better long-term decisions too. Why? Because they'd learned how to *wait for bigger rewards.*

Money works the same way. If you save and invest it, you can often end up with *more* than if you spend it right away.

Why it's important

When you understand the time value of money and the power of patience, you can:

- Make smarter choices with your money
- Avoid spending too quickly
- Grow your savings or investments over time
- Feel more in control of your future

Some of the smartest people in the world say this is *the* secret to long-term success.

Try this!

Pick something you want – maybe a toy or a treat. Now try waiting **one week** before buying it. Ask yourself: do you still want it just as much? Or did something better come along?

That's delayed gratification in action.

5

Risk and Reward

What it means to take a chance with money

What it means

Risk means there's a chance something might not go the way you hope. **Reward** is the good thing you get when it *does*.

In money, risk and reward often go together. If you take a big risk, you *might* get a big reward – but you could also lose something.

Smart money thinkers don't avoid risk completely. They just make sure the reward is *worth it* – and that they're prepared if things go wrong.

Here's an example

Let's say you've saved $10.

You could:

- Keep it safe in a piggy bank (low risk, small reward)
- Use it to buy candy and resell it at school for a small profit (medium risk, medium reward – if your friends actually buy it!)
- Buy raffle tickets hoping to win a new bike (high risk, high reward – but you'll likely walk away with nothing)

Each choice has a different level of **risk**, and a possible **reward**.

Why it's important

Understanding risk and reward helps you:

- Make smarter decisions with your money
- Know what you're comfortable losing
- Plan ahead for the best – and be ready for the worst
- Avoid putting *all* your money into risky ideas

In business and life, almost every smart move involves some level of risk. But with a clear plan and careful thinking, you can make it work for you – not against you.

Try this!

Make a list of three different things you could do with $10.

- Which one has the least risk?
- Which one has the most reward?
- Which one would *you* choose – and why?

There's no right answer. What matters is thinking it through.

Part 2

Earning
and Spending

Where money comes from, and where it goes

"A penny saved is a penny earned."
— Benjamin Franklin

Now that you know what money is and why it matters, it's time to look at how it moves. Because money doesn't just sit still – it's always going somewhere.

You can earn money by selling something, solving a problem, or doing a job. But once you've got it, you have to decide what to do with it – spend it, save it, or maybe a little of both. That's where the smart part comes in.

In this section, you'll learn:

- What it means to *earn* money, and why it feels so good
- What *expenses* are, and how they eat into your earnings
- How to figure out if you're actually making a *profit*
- Why *saving* helps you prepare for the future
- And how to *spend* wisely so you don't run out too fast

Ready to make some money moves?

6

Revenue

The money you make from selling something

What it means

Revenue is the total amount of money you make when someone buys something from you. It's the **first** money that comes in – before you subtract what you spent to make it.

Think of it as the top of the money mountain. You still have to climb down through costs and expenses to find out how much you actually *keep*, but **revenue** is where the climb starts.

Here's an example

Let's say you open a lemonade stand and sell cups for $1 each.

You sell:

- 3 cups to neighbors
- 2 to your friends
- 5 to your very thirsty grandma

That's 10 cups × $1 = **$10 in revenue**

You haven't counted your costs yet – just the total money that came in.

Why it's important

Revenue helps you:

- See if people are interested in what you're offering
- Measure how much money your product or service brings in
- Track growth over time (like, did you sell more this week than last week?)

Even if you're not making a profit yet, **revenue shows movement** – and that's how businesses begin.

Try this!

Sell something small (with permission!) – like a handmade bookmark or a snack. Keep track of what you sell and how much money you make. That's your **revenue** – and now you're in business!

7

Expenses

The money you spend to make or do something

What it means

Expenses are the things you pay for to make, sell, or do something.

If you're running a business – even a tiny one like a lemonade stand – you'll probably have to buy supplies, pay for space, or use tools. Those costs are called **expenses**.

They come **before** you figure out if you're actually making money.

Here's an example

You're selling lemonade for $1 a cup.

To make 10 cups, you buy:

- Lemons: $3
- Sugar: $1
- Cups: $2
- Poster board for your sign: $1

That's **$7 in expenses**.

Even if you make $10 in revenue, your **real earnings** don't start until after you subtract these costs.

Why it's important

Understanding expenses helps you:

- Know how much money you need to get started
- Avoid running out of money halfway through
- See how much you're really making (or losing)
- Make smarter choices about what's worth the cost

Even successful businesses have expenses – the smart ones *plan for them*.

Try this!

Ask a grown-up what they spent to make dinner tonight.

- Did they buy ingredients? Use gas or electricity?
- Was there a cost for time or effort?

That's the **real cost** of doing something – not just the money, but the thinking behind it.

8

Profit

What's left after the bills are paid

What it means

Profit is the money you have left over after you subtract your **expenses** from your **revenue**.

It's your **real earnings** – not just the money that came in, but what you actually get to keep.

Here's an example

Let's go back to your lemonade stand:

- You sell 10 cups for $1 each – that's **$10 in revenue**
- You spent $7 on lemons, sugar, cups, and poster board – that's **$7 in expenses**

So:

$10 revenue – $7 expenses = $3 profit

That $3 is your **reward** for doing the work and spending wisely.

Why it's important

Profit is what makes a business *worth doing*.

It helps you:

- Pay yourself for your time and effort
- Save up to grow your idea
- See if your business is really working
- Feel proud of what you've built

If your expenses are higher than your revenue, you don't make a profit – you take a loss. That's a sign it might be time to change something.

Try this!

Create your own pretend business – maybe a snack stand, pet-walking service, or comic book club. Write down what you'd sell, what you'd spend, and how much you'd charge. Now figure out your **profit**. Is it enough to make it worth your time?

9

Saving

Setting aside money for later

What it means

Saving means putting some of your money away now so you can use it **later** – when you really need or want it.

It's like pressing "pause" on your money. You're not spending it today, but it's still *yours* – just waiting for the right moment.

Here's an example

Let's say you earn $10.

You spend $6 on fun stuff now – a toy or a treat. But you **save $4** in a jar, bank, or account for something bigger – like a skateboard, a birthday gift for a friend, or even your future business.

That saved money is still working for you – just more *slowly and smartly*.

Why it's important

Saving helps you:

- Buy things you couldn't afford all at once
- Feel prepared for surprises (good or bad!)
- Make choices you're proud of – not just ones that feel good in the moment
- Become more independent and responsible with money

Even adults who earn lots of money still save – it's one of the smartest money moves around.

Try this!

Set a savings goal – like $20 for a game or gift.

Make a plan: how much will you save each week? Start today with whatever you've got – even $1 counts!

10

Spending

Choosing what to use your money for

What it means

Spending is what happens when you use your money to buy something – whether it's something you *need*, something you *want*, or something you're just really excited about right now.

But here's the trick: **you can't spend the same dollar twice**.

So smart spending means *choosing carefully*.

Here's an example

You have $10.

You could:

- Buy a pizza
- Go to the movies
- Save part of it and buy a smaller treat

Once you spend the money, it's gone – so every choice matters.

Spending is fun – but it's also a **decision**.

Why it's important

How you spend your money shows:

- What you value
- What you're thinking about (right now or in the future)
- Whether you're rushing into choices – or thinking things through

There's nothing wrong with spending – in fact, it's part of how money keeps moving. The key is spending on *purpose*, not just out of habit.

Try this!

Look at your last 3 purchases (or ask a grown-up what you spent money on this week). Would you make the same choices again? If not – what would you do differently next time?

That's how spending becomes smarter.

Part 3

Growing Your Money

How to make money earn more money… even while you sleep!

"Someone is sitting in the shade today because someone planted a tree a long time ago."
— Warren Buffett

What if your money could grow while you're sleeping? Or while you're playing outside? Or while you're doing *nothing at all*?

Good news – it can!

When you save, invest, or collect interest, your money starts working *for you*. Like a tiny employee in your wallet. The more you understand how this works, the smarter choices you can make with your money – and the faster it can grow.

In this section, you'll learn:

- What *interest* is and why banks pay you to save
- How *compound interest* can turn a little into a lot over time
- What it means to *invest* and how to grow your money with smart choices
- Why spreading your money out (*diversification*) keeps it safer
- And what banks actually *do* with your money when you hand it over

This is where your money brain levels up.

11

Interest

A reward for saving

What it means

Interest is extra money you earn just for keeping your money in a safe place – like a bank.

When you **save** money in a bank account, the bank actually pays **you** a little bit of money as a thank-you. That's interest.

Why? Because while your money is sitting in the bank, the bank uses it to help other people (like giving out loans). So they give you a small reward for letting it sit there.

Here's an example

Let's say you save **$100** in a bank.

If the bank gives you **2% interest**, that means you'll earn **$2** after one year – just for keeping your money there.

You didn't have to do anything. Your money just made more money by sitting still!

Why it's important

Interest is one of the easiest ways to:

- Grow your money slowly and safely
- Learn patience with saving
- Understand how money can work for you (not just the other way around)

Even small amounts can add up over time.

Try this!

Pretend you're starting your own bank. Create a simple chart to track how much money you're "saving" each week – even if it's just on paper.

Then imagine you earn **1% interest** each week. Use a calculator to add that extra bit to your savings. Watch how it grows – faster than you might expect!

That's interest in action.

12

Compound Interest

When your interest earns interest

What it means

Compound interest is when you earn interest not just on the money you saved – but also on the **interest you already earned**.

It's like getting a bonus on your bonus.

At first, it grows slowly. But over time, the amount starts to snow-ball – getting bigger and growing faster without you having to do anything extra.

Here's an example

Let's say you save **$100** in a bank account that gives you **5% inter-est** each year.

- After 1 year: You have $105 (because 5% of $100 = $5)
- After 2 years: You have $110.25 (because 5% of $105 = $5.25)
- After 3 years: You have even more – because now you're earning interest on **interest**

It's like planting a money seed that grows into a tree – and then that tree grows more trees!

Why it's important

Compound interest is one of the most powerful tools for growing money. It helps you:

- Grow savings faster the longer you wait
- Turn small amounts into bigger amounts
- Understand why **starting early** matters

Even grown-ups use this to plan for the future.

Try this!

Use a calculator to figure out how much money you'd have if you:

1. Saved $10
2. Earned 10% interest each year
3. Left it alone for 5 years

Don't spend a single dollar – just watch how it grows!

13

Investing

Making your money work for you

What it means

Investing means using your money to **buy something** that you think will grow in value or help you earn **even more money** later.

Instead of spending it on things that disappear (like snacks or games), you put your money into something that has the chance to **grow over time**.

That could be a business, a stock (part of someone else's business), real estate – or even your own skills!

Here's an example

Let's say you use your money to build a better lemonade stand.

You spend $50 on:

- A cooler to keep drinks colder
- A nicer sign to attract more customers
- Better ingredients to make tastier lemonade

If these things help you sell *more* lemonade or sell it at a higher price and make *more* profit, your $50 was a **smart investment**.

You took a risk – and it paid off.

Why it's important

Investing helps your money:

- Grow over time
- Work for you while you do other things
- Build wealth and reach bigger goals
- Teach you how to think long-term instead of short-term

It's not just about *having* money – it's about knowing how to **use it wisely**.

Try this!

Imagine you had $50 to invest in something. What would you choose? A lemonade stand? A lawn-mowing business? Art supplies to sell your work?

Think about:

- What you'd need to get started
- How you'd make your money back
- What could go wrong – and how you'd prepare

That's how an investor thinks.

14

Diversification

Don't put all your eggs (or coins) in one basket

What it means

Diversification means spreading your **money** across different investments so you're not taking one big risk.

If one thing doesn't go well, the others can help balance it out.

It's a way to **protect your savings** while still giving your money a chance to grow.

Here's an example

Let's say you invest all your money in one company – but it goes out of business. You lose everything.

Now imagine you split your money across **three different companies**. If one fails but the other two do well, your total money still grows.

That's diversification – it's about **not betting everything on one thing**.

Note! This works great with *money*, but not always with *time*. Spreading your energy across too many projects can make it harder to succeed. With your effort, focus is usually better!

Why it's important

Diversification helps you:

- Stay safer when investing
- Avoid losing everything if one idea goes badly
- Build a plan that can still grow, even when the world changes

It's how smart investors protect their future.

Try this!

Imagine you have $30 to invest.

- Would you put it all in one thing? Or split it up?
- What kinds of things would you pick?
- Which ones feel *safe*, and which ones feel *risky*?

That's how you start thinking like a wise investor.

15

How Banks Work

Where your money goes when you save it

What it means

When you put money in a **bank**, it doesn't just sit in a box with your name on it. The bank actually **uses** your money – safely and smartly – to help other people or businesses for a little while.

In return, they give you something back: **interest**.

Think of it like this: you're **lending your money to the bank**, and they're promising to keep it safe, pay you back, and add a little bonus for being patient.

Here's an example

Let's say you deposit $50 in a savings account.

The bank might use your money to help someone else buy a car, start a business, or fix up their house – all things that require a loan.

They charge that person interest on the loan, and then they **share a small part** of that interest with you. That's how your money earns money!

And don't worry – your money is protected and you can take it back when you need it.

Why it's important

Understanding how banks work helps you:

- Trust where your money is going
- See why saving in a bank is better than hiding it in a sock
- Learn how money moves through the economy
- Make smarter choices about **where** you keep your money

Saving at home keeps it safe. Saving at a bank helps it **grow**.

Try this!

Ask a grown-up if you can visit a real bank – or look one up online.

- What do they offer for saving money?
- How do savings accounts work?
- What questions would you ask if you were opening an account?

Banks aren't just for grown-ups – smart savers start early.

Part 4

Real-World Money

How money shows up all around you… and what you can do with it

*"It's not how much we give, but how much love
we put into giving."*
— Mother Teresa

By now, you know what money is, how to earn it, and even how to grow it. But what about the bigger picture?

Money doesn't live in a piggy bank forever – it moves through families, businesses, charities, and communities. The way people use money says a lot about what matters to them – not just what they can buy, but who they want to help and how they want to live.

In this section, you'll learn:

- The difference between *needs* and *wants* (and why it matters when you're spending)
- How kids like you can *earn* money in real life
- Why some people choose to *give* their money to help others
- What *businesses* do with their profits
- And why money can't buy *everything* – like kindness, fairness, or love

This is where you learn to use money with *heart* – not just with your wallet.

16

Needs vs. Wants

What really matters when you spend

What it means

Some things you buy are things you **need** – like food, water, clothes, and a place to live. Other things are things you **want** – like video games, candy, or the latest sneakers.

Needs help you live.

Wants help you have fun.

Both are okay – but knowing the difference helps you **spend smarter**.

Here's an example

Let's say you have $10.

You need to buy lunch at school – that's a **need**. You also want to buy a pack of trading cards – that's a **want**.

If you spend all your money on cards, you'll be hungry. But if you buy lunch first and still have money left, then the cards might be a smart choice.

Spending in the right order makes all the difference.

Why it's important

Knowing your **needs vs. wants** helps you:

- Make better spending choices
- Avoid running out of money for important stuff
- Feel more in control when money is tight
- Plan ahead for what really matters

Smart money thinkers always ask: *"Do I need this – or just want it?"*

Try this!

Make a list of 5 things you've spent money on this month. Next to each one, write **Need** or **Want**.

- How many were needs?
- How many were wants?
- Would you make any changes next time?

That's how smart spending begins.

17

Earning Money as a Kid

From chores to side hustles

What it means

You don't need to be a grown-up to start making money. Kids can earn money by doing helpful jobs, creating cool things, or solving problems for others.

The key is to think: **What can I do that someone else needs or wants?**

When you do that – and do it well – people are often happy to **pay you** for it.

Here's an example

You could earn money by:

- Doing extra chores at home
- Walking a neighbor's dog
- Selling homemade crafts or snacks
- Helping a relative organize their garage
- Starting a simple business, like a lemonade stand

You don't need to start big. Just start **helpful**.

Why it's important

Earning money helps you:

- Learn responsibility and confidence
- Understand what your time and effort are worth
- Save up for things you care about
- Feel proud of what you've built – even if it's small

Money that you **earn** often means more than money you're **given**.

Try this!

Make a list of 5 ways you could earn money in the next month. Then pick one and try it!

- What would you need?
- Who could you help?
- How much would you charge?

Start small – and grow from there.

18

Charity and Giving

Helping others
with what you've got

What it means

Giving is when you use your money to help someone else – not because you have to, but because you *want* to.

That could mean:

- Donating to a charity
- Buying supplies for someone in need
- Helping a friend or neighbor who's having a tough time

You don't need to be rich to give. You just need to **care**.

Here's an example

Let's say you earn $10 from your lemonade stand.

You decide to keep $6, save $2, and donate $2 to help rescue animals or buy food for a local shelter.

That $2 might not feel like much – but if lots of kids did that, it could make a **huge** difference.

Why it's important

Giving helps you:

- Build empathy and kindness
- Feel more connected to your community
- Use your money for something *bigger than yourself*
- Learn that the best rewards aren't always things you can buy

Money isn't just for getting – it's for **doing good**, too.

Try this!

Pick a cause that matters to you – animals, the environment, kids who need help, anything.

Then decide:

- How could you raise or set aside a small amount to donate?
- What else could you give? (Time? Kindness? Something you made?)
- How would it feel to give it?

That's how generosity begins.

19

How Businesses Use Money

What companies do with their earnings

What it means

When a business earns money, it doesn't just go straight into some-one's pocket. There are lots of smart ways businesses **use** their money to stay strong, grow, and keep customers happy.

After paying their **expenses**, businesses decide what to do with their **profit** – and every choice can shape what happens next.

Here's an example

Let's say your lemonade stand earns a profit of $10.

You could:

- Buy more lemons and sugar for tomorrow (to keep going)
- Save some in case you have a slow day (to stay safe)
- Invest in a bigger sign or a second table (to grow your stand)
- Give part to a good cause (to make a difference)
- Keep a little as a reward for yourself (you earned it!)

Big companies make similar choices – just with *way* more zeroes.

Why it's important

Understanding how businesses use money helps you:

- See how companies grow (or fail)
- Think like a smart business owner
- Make better choices in your own projects or side hustles
- Know where the money actually goes when you buy something

Smart businesses don't just make money – they **use it wisely**.

Try this!

Pretend you ran a lemonade stand and made $20 in profit. What would you do with the money?

Write down how much you'd put toward:

- Keeping it running
- Growing it
- Giving some away
- Saving it
- Paying yourself

That's a business budget in the making!

20

What Money Can't Do

Why values still matter

What it means

Money can do a lot of things – it can buy you food, clothes, toys, even time. But there are some things money **can't** do.

It can't buy friendship. It can't buy honesty or kindness. It can't make people respect you if you don't treat them well.

That's why **values** – the things you believe are right and important – matter even more than money.

Here's an example

Let's say you have enough money to buy any toy you want... but you don't share with your friends, or you brag, or you cheat to win.

Soon, people might not want to play with you – no matter how cool your stuff is.

Now imagine you *don't* have a lot of money... but you're helpful, generous, and fun to be around.

That's the kind of wealth that really lasts.

Why it's important

Knowing what money **can't** do helps you:

- Stay kind and humble, even when you succeed
- Make choices you'll feel proud of
- Focus on what really matters – not just what's expensive
- Be the kind of person others want to work with, play with, and trust

Money is a tool. **Character is who you are**.

Try this!

Think of someone you admire. Is it because they're rich? Or because they're kind, honest, funny, or brave?

Make a list of values that matter to *you*.

Then ask yourself: do my money choices reflect those values?

That's how money and meaning work together.

Business Brain Challenge
Can You Make $10 from Scratch?

You've learned a lot about how money works – now it's time to put that brain to work!

Your mission, if you choose to accept it, is to make $10 using what you've learned in this book.

You can earn it, save toward it, grow it, or even combine ideas – just make sure you track what you do and explain why.

Ready?

💡 Step 1: Think of an Idea

Start by brainstorming ways to earn money. You could:

- Sell something you make (bookmarks, bracelets, art)
- Offer a helpful service (dog walking, chores, organizing toys)
- Re-sell something with permission (garage sale or trading cards)

☑ Tip

Choose something *people want*, that you *enjoy doing*, and that doesn't require much money to get started.

🧮 Step 2: Plan Your Costs

- What supplies will you need?
- Will you have any *expenses*?
- How much will it cost you to make or do what you're offering?

Write down your estimated **expenses** and **set a price** for what you'll charge.

💲 Step 3: Track Your Revenue

As you start earning, keep a record of:

- What you sold or did
- How much you earned
- What you spent

🧠 Step 4: Did You Make a Profit?

Subtract your expenses from your revenue. That's your **profit**.

- Did you earn more than $10?
- Could you earn more if you kept going?
- What would you do differently next time?

🌱 Step 5: Decide What to Do with Your Money

Now that you've made some money:

- Will you **spend** it on something fun?
- Will you **save** it for something big?
- Will you **invest** it to grow even more?
- Will you **give** some away to help someone else?

There's no wrong answer – just make sure it's *your* decision.

☑ Your Business Brain Scorecard

Step	Done?	Notes
Idea brainstormed	☐	
Costs planned	☐	
Revenue tracked	☐	
Profit calculated	☐	
Spending/saving decision made	☐	

🎉 You did it!

Whether you made $2 or $200, you thought like a business brain. That's what **GrowForth Kids Co.** is all about.

Back-Pocket Bonuses

You made it! 🙌

You've just finished learning about how money works – how to earn it, grow it, save it, and use it wisely.

That's a big deal.

And now? You've officially earned your spot in the **GrowForth Kids Co. Hall of Brains**.

This section is full of extra goodies to keep in your back pocket (not your back *wallet* – those are for dollars, remember?).

Here's what you'll find:

- A **"What I Tried" Log** to track your experiments, challenges, and money moves
- A **Certificate of Completion** to prove you've got a money brain
- A **Glossary** with simple reminders of everything you've learned
- A little **Thank-You Note** from us
- And a quick peek **Behind the Book** to meet the authors and learn how this all came together

Take a moment to look back at what you've done.

And get ready to **Grow Forth**.

"What I Tried" Log

Your very own record of money missions, mini-businesses, and big ideas!

Try out something you learned in this book – like saving, selling, investing, or making a smart spending choice – then write about it here. You can use this log again and again as you grow your money brain!

Try #1

What I tried:

_____

What money skill did I use?

☐ Saving

☐ Earning

☐ Spending

☐ Giving

☐ Investing

☐ Other: _____

How did it go?

_____
_____

What did I learn?

_____
_____

Would I do it again?

☐ Yes

☐ No

☐ Maybe – but I'd do it differently.

Try #2

What I tried:

_____

What money skill did I use?

☐ Saving

☐ Earning

☐ Spending

☐ Giving

☐ Investing

☐ Other: _____

How did it go?

_____
_____

What did I learn?

_____
_____

Would I do it again?

☐ Yes

☐ No

☐ Maybe – but I'd do it differently.

Try #3

What I tried:

_____

What money skill did I use?

☐ Saving

☐ Earning

☐ Spending

☐ Giving

☐ Investing

☐ Other: _____

How did it go?

_____
_____

What did I learn?

_____
_____

Would I do it again?

☐ Yes

☐ No

☐ Maybe – but I'd do it differently.

Try #4

What I tried:

_____

What money skill did I use?

☐ Saving

☐ Earning

☐ Spending

☐ Giving

☐ Investing

☐ Other: _____

How did it go?

_____
_____

What did I learn?

_____
_____

Would I do it again?

☐ Yes

☐ No

☐ Maybe – but I'd do it differently.

Try #5

What I tried:

_____

What money skill did I use?

- ☐ Saving
- ☐ Earning
- ☐ Spending
- ☐ Giving
- ☐ Investing
- ☐ Other: _____

How did it go?

_____
_____

What did I learn?

_____
_____

Would I do it again?

- ☐ Yes
- ☐ No
- ☐ Maybe – but I'd do it differently.

GrowForth Kids Co.

Certificate of Completion

Official Proof of Awesomeness

CERTIFICATE OF
COMPLETION

Official Proof of Awesomeness

has officially completed:

Book 1:
How Money
Works

CERTIFIFED BUSINESS BRAIN

They've explored what money is, how it works, how to grow it, and how to use it wisely. They've thought, planned, saved, earned, and maybe even launched a brilliant idea.

Most of all, they've shown that they're ready to *Grow Forth*.

Glossary
Big Words Made Simple

Bank: A safe place where people keep their money and sometimes earn interest.

Book Value: What something *originally* cost or is officially worth on paper.

Compound Interest: When you earn interest on your money *and* on the interest you already earned.

Diversification: Spreading your money across different investments so you're not putting it all in one place.

Earning: Getting money by doing something helpful, useful, or valuable.

Expenses: The money you spend to make or do something (like buying lemons for a lemonade stand).

Giving: Using your money to help others, not because you have to – but because you want to.

Inflation: When prices go up over time, so money doesn't buy as much as it used to.

Interest: A reward (extra money) you get for saving or letting someone else use your money for a while.

Investing: Using your money to buy something that could grow in value or make more money later.

Market Value: What something is worth *right now*, based on what someone would actually pay for it.

Needs: Things you *must* have to live (like food, water, and clothes).

Profit:	The money you have left after you subtract your expenses from your revenue.
Revenue:	The total money you make from selling something before paying for any expenses.
Risk:	The chance that something won't go as planned, and you might lose money.
Reward:	The good thing you get when something *does* go as planned – like making a profit.
Saving:	Setting money aside to use later, instead of spending it right away.
Spending:	Using money to buy something, whether it's a need or a want.
Values:	The things you believe are important – like kindness, fairness, or helping others.
Wants:	Things you *like*, but don't *need* to live (like toys, treats, or gadgets).

A Thank-You from GrowForth Kids Co.

Hey there, Business Brain!

We just wanted to say a **huge THANK YOU** for spending time with this book – for thinking, learning, planning, trying, and growing your money smarts one page at a time.

You didn't just read about money.

You *understood* it. You *used* it. You *owned* it.

And that's a big deal.

Remember:

- 💡 You don't have to wait to be a grown-up to make smart money moves.
- 🐽 You already have everything you need to start.
- 🌱 And the more you practice, the more your money brain will grow.

Whether you earned your first dollar, saved for something special, or helped someone else with what you've got – we're proud of you.

Stay curious. Stay generous.

And keep growing forth.

See you in the next book!

— Your friends at **GrowForth Kids Co.**

Behind the Book

Meet the Authors

Hi! We're **Matthew** and **Scott MacMillan** – a father-and-son duo from Toronto, Canada who teamed up to write this book together.

Scott (the dad!) is an entrepreneur, former Boston Consulting Group (BCG) strategy consultant, and the author of *Entrepreneur to Author*. He now runs a publishing company that helps experts turn their ideas into books that grow their business (Parents, learn more at: www.grammarfactory.com).

Matthew (the kid!) is full of clever ideas, sharp questions, and curious thinking – especially about money, business, and how the world works. He's also the author of *The Super Poo Official Character Guide*, which launched his own creative publishing journey.

One day, Matthew asked something simple but smart:

"How does a business work?"

That kicked off a ton of conversations – about saving, earning, running a business, and making smart decisions. The more we talked, the more we realized: this stuff isn't just for grown-ups. In fact, kids who learn these ideas early can use them to do some pretty amazing things. So we decided to write the kind of book we both wish existed earlier – clear, fun, and full of real tools for thinking like a **business brain**.

This is just the beginning. We've got a whole series planned – and we hope you'll come along for the ride.

Thanks for reading, learning, and growing with us!

— **Matthew & Scott**

Want to keep up with the latest books, tools, and challenges from Grow-Forth Kids Co.? Visit **www.growforthpress.com** to stay in the loop!

You Might Also Like...

If you liked Book 1, *How Money Works*, we've got good news – the journey is just beginning!

Here's a sneak peek at the other books in the **GrowForth Kids Co. Business Brain Series**:

Book 1 (That's THIS book!)

How Money Works: Learn How to Earn It, Save It, Grow It, and Spend It Wisely

Learn the basics of money: what it is, how it works and how to use it. Topics: Revenue, expenses, profit, giving, values, and more.

Book 2 (Coming Soon!)

Smart Choices: The Economics of Everyday Decisions

Learn to make better choices with your time, money, and energy. Topics: Opportunity cost, sunk cost, marginal thinking, tradeoffs, and more.

Book 3

Let's Start a Business! Your First Steps into Entrepreneurship

Discover how to launch and run a simple business (like a lemonade stand... but smarter!). Topics: Break-even point, marketing, USP, sales, and scaling.

Book 4

Team Up! How People Work Together to Get Big Things Done

Explore what makes teamwork work – and how different strengths can build something great. Topics: Division of labor, KPIs, public goods, comparative advantage, and more.

Book 5

Thinking Like a Business Brain: Mindset, Strategy & Making an Impact

Learn how to think like a leader – with purpose, ethics, and long-term thinking. Topics: Strategy vs. tactics, innovation, risk, continuous improvement, and values.

...and that's only the first 5 book! Big things are coming...

Want to know when the next book is out?

Visit **www.growforthpress.com** to explore upcoming titles, get free resources, and join the GrowForth Kids Co. community.